Copyright 2010 by Realistic Tones

Happy Easter

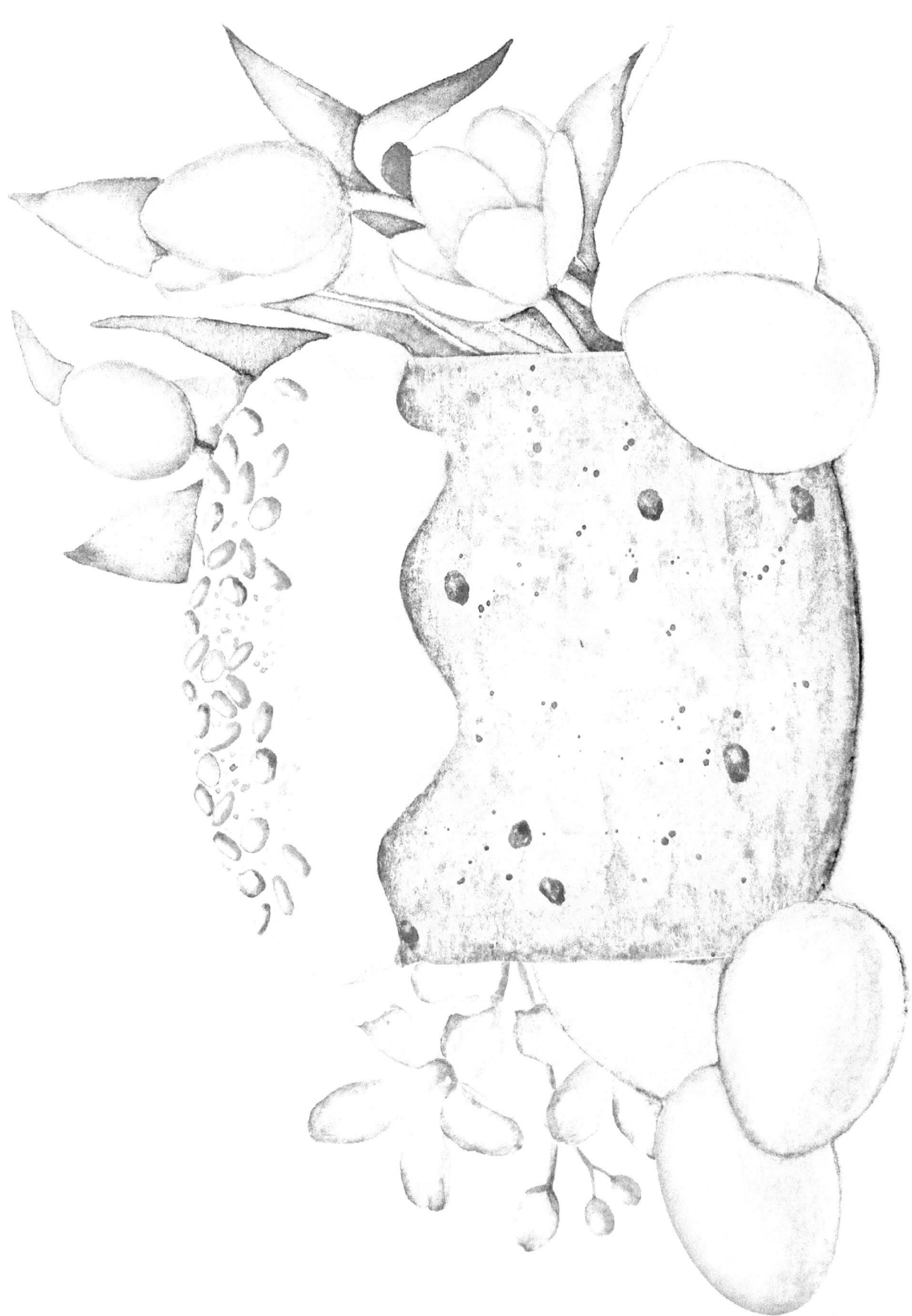

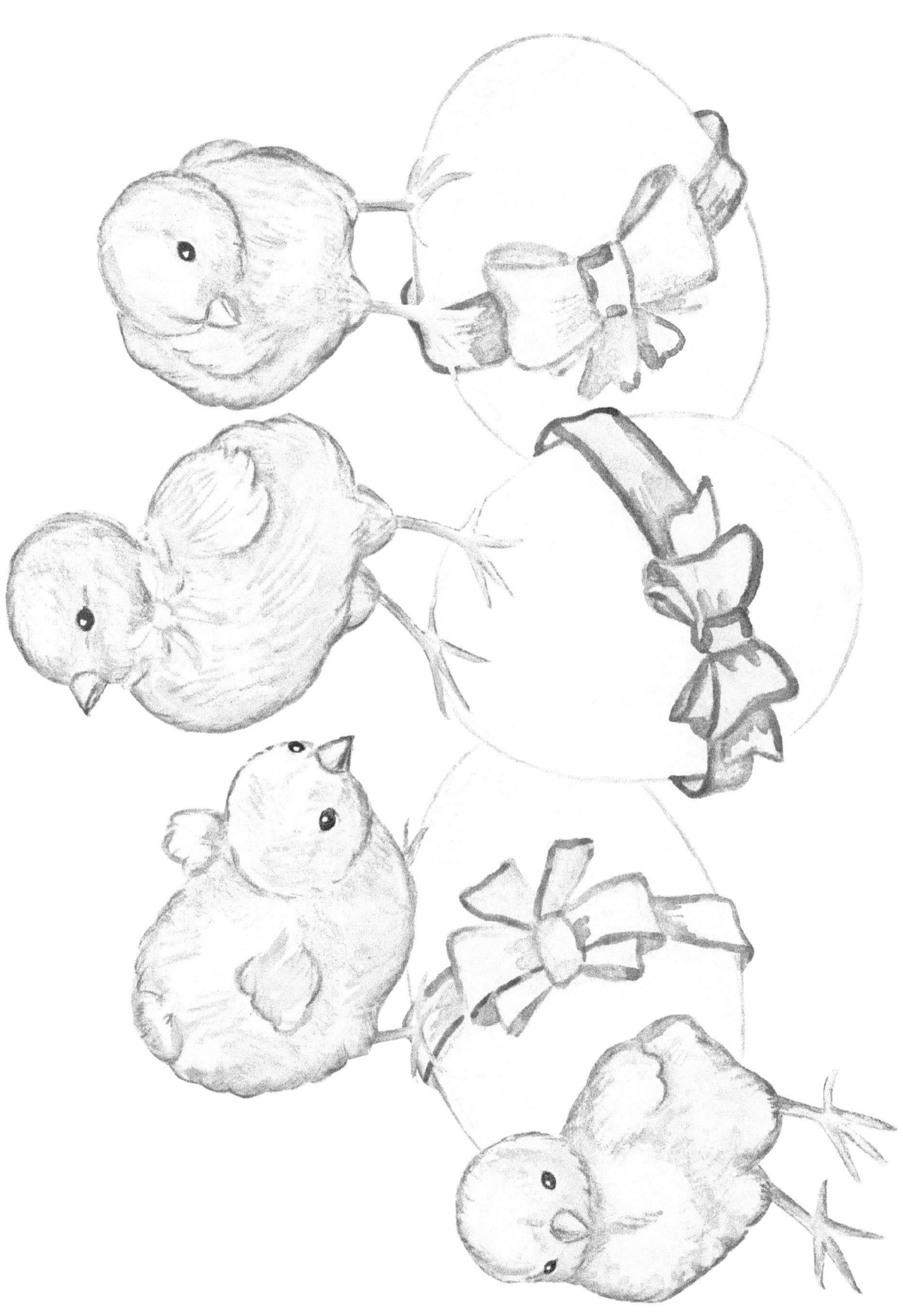

Realistic grayscale coloring books for adults: BIRDS

Bird
Coloring book
FOR ADULTS

REALISTIC *Tones*

www.ingramcontent.com/pod-product-compliance
Lightning Source LLC
LaVergne TN
LVHW060218080526
838202LV00052B/4299